Taj Mahal

BY ELIZABETH RAUM

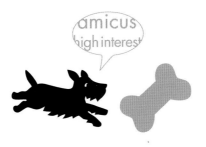

amicus
high interest

Amicus High Interest is an imprint of Amicus
P.O. Box 1329, Mankato, MN 56002
www.amicuspublishing.us

Library of Congress Cataloging-in-Publication Data
Raum, Elizabeth.
Taj Mahal / by Elizabeth Raum.
    pages cm. — (Ancient wonders)
 Summary: "Describes the Taj Mahal, including how and why it
was built, how it was ruined and has been restored, and what it
is like today"—Provided by publisher.
 Includes bibliographical references.
 ISBN 978-1-60753-470-9 (library binding) —
 ISBN 978-1-60753-685-7 (ebook)
1. Taj Mahal (Agra, India) —Juvenile literature. 1. Title.
 DS486.A3R38 2015
 954'.2—dc23

                                    2013028302

Editors   Kristina Ericksen and Rebecca Glaser
Series Designer Kathleen Petelinsek
Book Designer   Heather Dreisbach
Photo Researcher Kurtis Kinneman

Photo Credits: Alamy, 6, 9, 10, 13, 19, 20; Getty Images, 16,
23; Mary Evans Picture Library, 14; Shutterstock, cover, 5, 24,
29; Superstock, 26

Printed in the United States of America at Corporate Graphics
in North Mankato, Minnesota.

10 9 8 7 6 5 4 3 2 1

Table of Contents

A Beautiful Building 4

A Love Story 8

Building the Taj Mahal 14

Falling into Ruin 22

The Taj Mahal Today 27

Glossary 30

Read More 31

Websites 31

Index 32

A Beautiful Building

The Taj Mahal is the one of the most famous buildings in the world. Stone paths lead up to it. Huge gardens surround it. Towers called **minarets** stand at each corner. A long pool shaped like a rectangle acts like a mirror. It reflects the Taj in its clear waters.

A long pool leads up to the Taj Mahal.

The Taj Mahal is in Agra, India. It sits at the edge of the Yumuna River. Agra was part of the **Mughal** Empire. It included northern India, Pakistan, Afghanistan, and Kashmir. The empire lasted from 1526 to 1858. The Mughals built beautiful buildings and gardens. They built the Taj Mahal. Why? Its story begins with a Mughal love story.

The Taj Mahal overlooks the Yumuna River in India.

A Love Story

In 1607, a handsome young Mughal prince went to the royal market. As he was looking at jewelry, he noticed a young girl. She was more beautiful than the most precious gems. The prince stopped and spoke to her. He fell in love. So did she. Five years later, they married.

The prince married the lovely
girl he met at the royal market.

In 1628, the prince became **emperor**. He was called Shah Jahan. Some called him the "King of the World." His wife was named Mumtaz Mahal. She was called "the Chosen One of the Palace." They spent all their time together. They helped each other in many ways. They were deeply in love.

Mumtaz Mahal became queen. She ruled with her husband, the emperor.

Shah Jahan and Mumtaz Mahal had 13 children. In 1630, Mumtaz gave birth to their fourteenth child, a baby girl. Then Mumtaz fell ill. The shah rushed to her side. She lay dying. She whispered a last wish. She wanted him to build her the world's most beautiful **tomb**.

 Did she really ask for a beautiful tomb?

The tombs in the Taj Mahal are empty. The real graves are in a lower level.

A Many believe she did. We'll never know for sure.

Building the Taj Mahal

After Mumtaz died, the shah began to plan her tomb. He chose the site. He bought the land. He hired **architects** to design the tomb. They made careful measurements. They drew building plans. The shah chose two men to lead the project. They hired the best workers in the land.

Shah Jahan spent all his time planning the Taj Mahal after his wife died.

The domes were built with bricks and covered with marble.

 Q How did the workers move heavy marble?

Workers built a base near the river. Then they built brick walls. They layered the bricks higher and higher to form the outside walls.

They made the domes with bricks, too. Workers laid them in circles. Each layer was built higher and closer together to form a dome. Workers covered the bricks with marble.

Elephants and oxen pulled it on wagons. It came from 250 miles (402 km) away.

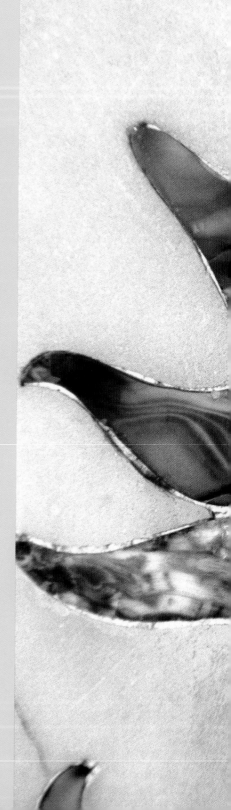

The shah ordered stones from far away. Crystal and jade came from China. Turquoise came from Turkey. Shells and coral came from the Indian Ocean.

Stonecutters prepared the stones. Artists used them to make **mosaics** for inside the Taj Mahal.

Artists made detailed pictures from polished stones.

Poems from the Koran were written on the walls in Arabic.

Q How long did it take to build the Taj Mahal?

Shah Jahan hired **calligraphers** to write poetry on the walls. **Calligraphy**, or decorative writing, is an art. The poems used in the Taj Mahal come from the Koran. It is the holy book of the Islam religion.

Gardens surround the Taj Mahal. They line the walkways. There are 64 gardens. Each has 400 plants.

 It took 20,000 workers 22 years.

Falling into Ruin

Shah Jahan died in 1666. He was buried in the Taj Mahal next to Mumtaz. The Mughals ruled India until the 1850s. Then the British took control.

After that, the Taj Mahal fell into ruin. People had parties there. They took jewels off the walls. The gardens grew wild. The British planned to tear down the Taj Mahal.

 Why did they want to tear it down?

The Taj Mahal was well preserved until the 1850s.

A They wanted to sell the marble. The stone was popular in England.

The gardens at the Taj Mahal have been restored.

Then two things happened. First, word came to India that marble was not selling well. No one wanted to buy it. Second, in 1899, George Curzon came to India. Curzon was a British official. He loved the Taj Mahal. He hired workers to fix it up. They cleaned the marble. They replanted the gardens. The Taj Mahal was beautiful again.

The Taj Mahal Today

Today, **air pollution** is a problem for the Taj Mahal. India uses coal to run factories. Coal makes dirty smoke. The smoke damages the white marble. In 1996, the government banned the use of coal near the Taj Mahal. Many factories switched to gas. Others moved farther away.

Morning mist hangs in the air around the Taj Mahal.

Every year, two to four million people visit the Taj Mahal. About 200,000 come from other countries. Cars are not allowed. Tourists walk from parking lots or take an electric bus. They are eager to see the Taj Mahal. It is one of the world's greatest wonders.

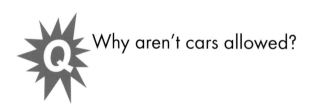
Why aren't cars allowed?

The marble on the Taj Mahal
seems to change color
when the light changes.

A The Indian government wants to protect
the Taj Mahal. Cars make too much pollution

Glossary

air pollution Dirty or unhealthy air caused by factories, cars, or other factors.

architect A person who designs buildings.

calligrapher An artist who does decorative writing.

calligraphy Decorative writing.

emperor A ruler or king.

minaret A tower that is taller than it is wide.

mosaic A picture or design made by setting small colored gems or pieces of stone into a surface.

Mughal A family who ruled areas of northern India, Pakistan, Afghanistan, and Kashmir between 1526 and 1858.

tomb A burial chamber or monument used as a grave.

Read More

Henzel, Cynthia Kennedy. *Taj Mahal*. Edina, Minn.: ABDO Pub. Co., 2011.

Kissock, Heather. *Taj Mahal*. New York: AV2 by Weigl, 2012.

Riggs, Kate. *Taj Mahal*. Mankato, Minn.: Creative Education, 2009.

Websites

Official Website of the Taj Mahal
http://tajmahal.gov.in/

Taj Mahal—Emperor Shah Jahan—Great Buildings Architecture
http://www.greatbuildings.com/buildings/ Taj_Mahal.html

Taj Mahal—World Heritage Site—National Geographic
http://travel.nationalgeographic.com/travel/ world-heritage/taj-mahal/

Every effort has been made to ensure that these websites are appropriate for children. However, because of the nature of the Internet, it is impossible to guarantee that these sites will remain active indefinitely or that their contents will not be altered.

Index

architects 14
calligraphy 21
Curzon, George 25
dome 17
gardens 4, 7, 21, 22, 25
gems 8, 18
Jahan, Shah 11, 12, 21, 22
Mahal, Mumtaz 11, 12,
  14, 22

marble 16–17, 23, 25, 27
minarets 4
mosaics 18
Mughals 7, 8, 22
pollution 27, 29
repair 25
tourists 28

About the Author

Elizabeth Raum has worked as a teacher, librarian, and writer. She has written dozens of books for young readers. She likes doing research and learning about new topics. After writing about ancient wonders, she wants to travel the world to visit them! To learn more, visit her website at www.elizabethraum.net.